Christmas

IS COMING

D1717173

1 2 3 4 5 6

7 8 9 10 11 12

13 14 15 16 17 18

19 20 21 22 23 24

 25

20

Dear Customer

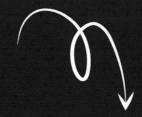

Thank you for your recent purchase. We hope you love it! If you do, would you consider posting an online review?

This helps us to continue providing great products and helps potential buyers to make confident decisions.

Thank you in advance for your review and for being a preferred customer.

Illustrations:
CANVA
VECTEEZY
PIXABAY

Made in the USA
Middletown, DE
04 November 2021

51698731R00031